MENTAL HEALTH AND TRAUMA AFTER THE STORM:

A TRIBUTE TO THE AFFECTED AREAS OF JAMAICA

KAMELAH BLAIR

Copyright © 2025 by Kamelah Blair

All rights reserved. No part of this book may be used or reproduced in any form whatsoever without written permission except in the case of brief quotations in critical articles or reviews.

Printed in the United States of America and or Canada

For more information, or to book an event, contact :
Email:info@royaltyhelpinghands.com

Book design by COJ BOOKZ
 Paperback: ISBN: 978-1-998120-97-0

Opening Letter: A Hug, A Smile, and Continuous Prayers

To My Beloved Jamaica,

My heart aches with yours, for the homes lost, the land scarred, and the stillness that has replaced the rhythmic noise of everyday life. In this moment of profound loss and quiet devastation, I want to send you the biggest hug, a warm smile, and my continuous prayers. You are built on the bedrock of resilience. Your history, your culture, your very soul is a testament to the strength that can endure any blow. You are the mango tree that loses its limb but sends forth a green, defiant shoot.

But, beloved Jamaica, in the immediate aftermath, that strength doesn't mean you must be stone. This is not the time for just "tek set." It is okay to be vulnerable. It is okay to weep for the roof you lost and the memories washed away. It is okay to feel the fear.

Trauma leaves an invisible mark, and healing is not a race; it is a journey we take together. This book is a dedication to your survival, a validation of your pain, and a guide to tending to the precious, resilient heart of your people. We are here. We remember. We will rebuild, one soul at a time.

With all my love and faith,

Kamelah Blair

CHAPTER 1

Part I: The Immediate Storm Within

(The First Month)

The Roar and the Aftershock: Day Zero

The hurricane is not just wind and rain; it is noise. A terrifying, relentless roar that threatens to tear the very foundations from beneath your feet. For many in our affected areas, the memory of that sound—that primal, sustained shriek—remains the deepest wound of all.
Understanding the Body's Defense: Shock and Numbness
In those first hours and days, your body and mind were focused solely on survival. If you found yourself moving slowly, unable to cry, or simply focused on picking up one piece of debris after another without feeling much of anything, that was your body's built-in defense mechanism known as shock or numbness.

Simple Explanation: Shock is like an emergency power-down button for your feelings. Your brain recognized the threat was too big and too overwhelming to process all at once, so it temporarily shut down your major emotional circuits. It is a protective, normal reaction to an abnormal, terrifying event.

Real-Life Example: Think of Miss Mavis from Clarendon. When her roof blew off, she didn't scream or cry. Instead, she spent the next three hours calmly sweeping the water and broken glass into neat piles, telling her neighbour she was just "waiting for the sun to come out." It wasn't until a week later, when a song came on the radio, that the tears finally came. Miss Mavis's initial calmness was not strength; it was shock protecting her heart until she was safe enough to feel the loss.

Acute Stress: When Safety Doesn't Feel Safe

As the immediate danger passes, the mind starts trying to make sense of what happened. For many, the fear doesn't disappear when the sun comes out. It transforms into Acute Stress Disorder (ASD).

Simple Explanation: Acute Stress Disorder describes the intense, disruptive anxiety, fear, and feeling of being on edge that lasts anywhere from three days up to one month after the trauma. If you have been jumping at the sound of heavy rain or even a loud truck driving by, that is a classic symptom of ASD known as hyper-vigilance. Your nervous system is stuck in "high alert."

The Data Validates You: Researchers who study communities after disasters know that these feelings are not unique. For example, studies following severe storms show that intrusive thoughts, where the person keeps reliving the scariest moment, are present in a significant majority of affected people immediately following the event. Your fear is a real wound that needs tending.

Real-Life Example: Little Michael in Portland might refuse to sleep in his own room, insisting on sleeping under the dining table. When his father asks why, Michael can only point to the table and say, "It's strong." Michael is experiencing avoidance and hyper-arousal. He is avoiding the place where he felt vulnerable, and his body is seeking out perceived structural safety, even after the storm is over.

This is a common sign of ASD in children—they often don't have the words, so their actions speak their fear.

It is crucial to understand that if these intense feelings and fears last less than one month, they are categorized as Acute Stress Disorder. It is a powerful message of hope because for most people, the mind successfully processes the event, and these symptoms naturally begin to fade within that time. We call this natural recovery.

CHAPTER 2
The First Grief: When Home is Gone

The storm takes more than just roofs and windows; it takes a sense of certainty. When we lose our home, we lose the anchor of our identity and safety. In the first few weeks after the disaster, the grief that hits is overwhelming, often coming in unpredictable waves. It's not just grief for a life lost; it's grief for the life that was. The Loss of "Sense of Place" For many Jamaicans, the home is everything—it is where generations are raised, where family history resides, and where community is centered. The trauma of displacement, or seeing your sacred space reduced to rubble, is profound.

Simple Explanation: We are wired to feel safe in familiar places. When that environment is destroyed, our brain interprets the loss as a complete violation of safety. This results in feelings of intense anxiety, rootlessness, and despair, often more keenly felt than the loss of objects themselves. The psychological loss of the environment is called "Solastalgia," or distress caused by environmental change.

Real-Life Example: Mr. George, who lived in the same small house in St. Thomas his entire life, was rescued after a flood. Weeks later, he was safe, but he could not stop pacing. He was healthy, but he felt sick. He kept saying, "Mi cyant sleep easy because mi home nah hold mi." His fear wasn't about the storm returning; it was the pain of losing the only physical representation of his stability and lineage. That lack of "holding" is the loss of a physical security blanket.

Unpredictable Grief and the Community Response

Grief in the aftermath of a disaster is often not neat or linear. It can be intense sadness over losing a life, but it can also be a sudden burst of tears over finding a damaged family photo, or fierce anger over a ruined garden.

The Data Validates You: Following major disasters, studies show that nearly 50% of the affected population experiences significant early grief symptoms. The loss of possessions and property is a huge factor, as these items are often irreplaceable and tied to identity.

Community Mobilization: In the absence of immediate official aid, the initial healing almost always comes from within. The instinctive Jamaican practice of communal support—neighbours pooling resources, the local shopkeeper offering credit, or the church opening its doors—is the first, most powerful mental health defense. It combats isolation, which is the fuel for chronic trauma.

CHAPTER 3

Part II: The Invisible Mark (Months 1 to 12)

The Second Storm: The Trauma of Livelihood Disruption

The wind may have stopped, but the worry has just begun. For many, the true measure of the disaster is not the cost of the repair, but the loss of the ability to earn a living. This sustained stress is what we call The Second Storm, and it is directly linked to mental health decline.

The Weight of Financial Loss and Identity

In Jamaica, like many places, a person's dignity is tied closely to their ability to provide for their family. When that ability is instantly wiped out—a fisherman's boat gone, a farmer's crops ruined—the psychological effect is devastating.

Simple Explanation: This trauma is rooted in the feeling of powerlessness. When external forces (the storm) make it impossible for you to fulfill your core role as a provider, it triggers deep feelings of shame, anxiety, and worthlessness. This persistent financial stress is a constant irritant that stops the initial psychological wounds from healing.

The Data Validates You: Research is clear: the single most reliable predictor of long-term mental health problems (like chronic depression and PTSD) after a disaster is hurricane-related financial loss and post-disaster stressors like housing and employment struggles. The data tells us that economic stress often outlasts the emotional shock of the storm itself.

Real-Life Example: Mr. Fitzroy, a respected farmer in St. Elizabeth, was devastated not by the damage to his house, but by the loss of his entire yield of scallions and tomatoes. He became withdrawn and silent. The shame of having to accept donated food, when he was usually the one providing for others, sent him into a profound depression. His family noticed he stopped sitting on the veranda—a sign of his withdrawal from the community, a direct result of losing his occupational identity.

CHAPTER 4

The Long Wait and The Erosion of Hope

After the adrenaline of survival wears off, people face the grinding reality of rebuilding. This phase is characterized by chronic stress—the exhausting, months-long struggle with bureaucracy, insurance claims, and living amidst perpetual clean-up. This "state of limbo" erodes hope.

The Psychological Toll of Limbo
The effort required just to get back to "normal" is often an invisible form of psychological trauma.

Simple Explanation: Living in a state of chronic stress means your body's alarm system never turns off. The initial symptoms of Acute Stress Disorder transition into General Anxiety Disorder and Depression. You become constantly tired, easily frustrated, and feel like you're waiting for the next disaster to strike.

The Data Validates You: Studies in the Caribbean confirm that distress is not short-lived. Some findings indicated persistently high levels of emotional distress in hurricane-affected communities nearly nine months after a storm. This confirms that the healing process is measured in months, not weeks, and that feeling depleted long after the event is real and valid.

Real-Life Example: Ms. Shirley from Kingston spent six months patching a tarp on her roof while waiting for aid assessments. She developed intense insomnia and began having severe emotional outbursts over small issues, like a bus being late.

This was not laziness or weakness; it was cumulative fatigue and chronic stress finally breaking through her emotional defenses. The stress of the wait was more damaging than the storm itself.

CHAPTER 5

The Hidden Coping: Substance Use and Conflict

When people feel overwhelmed, they often look for immediate escape or relief, which can lead to negative coping mechanisms. We must address the rise in self-medication and community tension with compassion and honesty.

Muting the Pain
The fear, stress, and unresolved grief are powerful motivators for people to seek relief, which often comes in the form of increased alcohol consumption or misuse of substances.

Simple Explanation: Alcohol and drugs provide temporary relief by chemically numbing the hyper-vigilance and anxiety that the trauma has created. However, this is a dangerous cycle: the substance only delays the emotional processing, leading to more severe depression and addiction later.

The Data Validates You: Research conducted across areas affected by mass trauma in the Caribbean confirms that there is an observable increase in alcohol-related problems and instances of reliance on substances as a coping mechanism, particularly among those who have lost their livelihoods or been displaced. This is a common consequence of trauma that requires clinical intervention, not judgment.

Real-Life Example: After the storm, John in Westmoreland started drinking heavily every afternoon, saying it was the only way to "stop the head-noise" of worry about the repairs. His withdrawal and increasing irritation at home led to arguments with his spouse, placing strain on his family life. This is a common and tragic ripple effect: the storm didn't damage his marriage, but his unmanaged stress did.

The Rise of Conflict
The extreme stress from loss and displacement acts as a fuel for existing tensions, often leading to increased frustration and even domestic conflict.

Simple Explanation: When resources are scarce, and everyone is emotionally exhausted, patience wears thin. Homes are crowded, money is tight, and the constant feeling of insecurity heightens aggressive responses.

The Data Validates You: Global studies on disaster impact consistently show that periods of high stress, displacement, and economic instability are risk factors for increased community and domestic violence. Recognizing this is the first step toward intervention and restoring stability.

Part III: The Enduring Heart (Beyond 1 Year and Into the Future)

CHAPTER 6

When The Shadow Lingers: Understanding PTSD

If the debilitating symptoms discussed in Parts I and II do not fade after several months, they may be classified as Post-Traumatic Stress Disorder (PTSD). This is not a lifetime sentence; it is a clinical term for a wound that needs specialized healing.

Recognizing the Lingering Shadow
The difference between acute stress and PTSD is persistence. If the symptoms of terror, avoidance, and fear continue to dominate life beyond a month, the trauma is likely now consolidated.

Simple Explanation: PTSD is your brain getting stuck in the past. It constantly believes the danger is still present, even when you are physically safe. It has four main ways of expressing itself:

Intrusion: Flashbacks, nightmares, or the storm suddenly feeling like it's happening again.

Avoidance: Deliberately avoiding anything that reminds you of the storm (rain, news reports, the location).

Negative Thoughts: Persistent negative beliefs about yourself ("I should have done more") or the world ("The future is hopeless").

Hyper-arousal: Being constantly on edge, easily startled, and having difficulty concentrating or sleeping.

The Data Validates You: While initial recovery rates are high, studies after major storms have indicated that a significant portion of the population (often ranging from 10% to 19%) may continue to experience clinical levels of PTSD or severe depression symptoms years later. This is why long-term resources are essential.

Real-Life Example: A young woman from Montego Bay found that every time the sky turned dark, she became convinced a new storm was coming, suffering intense, physical panic attacks (Intrusion/Hyper-arousal). She stopped watching the weather, avoiding the news completely (Avoidance). When this pattern persisted for over a year, she was experiencing PTSD. The key to healing for her was accepting that her body was reacting to a memory, not the present reality.

CHAPTER 7

Sankofa and the Soul of Revival

This chapter is the tribute—a celebration of the deep, enduring, and creative ways that Jamaica heals itself. The term Sankofa, though Akan, powerfully reflects the Jamaican spirit: looking to the past to inform the present. We look to our cultural practices not just for tradition, but for therapy.
Cultural Healing Mechanisms
The resources we need are often right here, embedded in our community fabric. The Power of Faith: For many, the church is the first therapist. The ritual, the communal prayer, and the affirmation of a higher power provide a framework for enduring suffering and finding meaning in loss.

Communal Labour and Partner: The healing power of doing. The act of neighbors pooling resources and physical effort to rebuild one home at a time is profoundly therapeutic. It restores the sense of community control that the storm took away.

The Music and the Word: Jamaican music, from spirituals to conscious reggae, often speaks to struggle, resilience, and hope. Storytelling and the creation of new songs are ways to process trauma collectively, turning pain into narrative and affirmation.

Real-Life Example: After a devastating flood, a small town in Hanover organized weekly "yard clean-up days" where 30 people would focus on one family's yard.
They called it "Grounding and Giving." This act of collective, physical support reduced individual anxiety, fostered mutual dependency, and was, in effect, community-led group therapy. The movement was the therapy.

CHAPTER 8

Building Stronger Minds: Lessons for the Next Storm

The greatest tribute we can offer is ensuring that the next generation is better prepared, not just for the winds, but for the psychological aftermath. Healing is about preparation.
  Integration of Mental Health: We must demand that disaster preparedness plans include immediate and sustained Mental Health and Psychosocial Support (MHPSS). This means training community leaders, teachers, and health workers in Psychological First Aid (PFA) before the storm hits.

A Call for Policy: The book concludes by calling on leaders to prioritize
long-term, accessible mental health infrastructure in rural and hard-hit areas, recognizing that the trauma budget must be as important as the rebuilding budget. Resource Page: Mind, Body, and Spirit

Immediate Mental Health and Counseling Support
If you or someone you know is experiencing persistent distress, please reach out. Remember, this is a sign of courage, not weakness.

Start with Your Community Health Center: Your nearest local clinic is the essential first step. They can offer screening and referrals to counselors and social workers.

National Mental Health Helpline: (Placeholder for specific, confirmed National Mental Health Helpline Numbers within

Jamaica). Please seek out the most current, public government mental health hotline.

Seek Trusted Counsel: Talk to your Pastor, Church Elder, or a respected leader in your community. These figures are vital sources of wisdom and initial emotional support.
Actionable Coping Strategies

"The storm was strong, but our roots are deeper. It may have stripped the leaves, but it could not touch the soul. And just like the land we love, we were built to bloom again.
We are not defined by the wreckage we stand in, but by the hands we hold while we rebuild. The wind has passed, but the people remain.
We are little, but we are Tallawah."

MY HEALING NOTES

MY HEALING NOTES

MY HEALING NOTES

MY HEALING NOTES

MY HEALING NOTES

MY HEALING NOTES

MY HEALING NOTES

MY HEALING NOTES

MY HEALING NOTES

MY HEALING NOTES

MY HEALING NOTES

MY HEALING NOTES

MY HEALING NOTES

MY HEALING NOTES

MY HEALING NOTES

MY HEALING NOTES

MY HEALING NOTES

MY HEALING NOTES

MY HEALING NOTES

MY HEALING NOTES

MY HEALING NOTES

MY HEALING NOTES

MY HEALING NOTES

MY HEALING NOTES

MY HEALING NOTES

MY HEALING NOTES

MY HEALING NOTES

www.ingramcontent.com/pod-product-compliance
Lightning Source LLC
Chambersburg PA
CBHW071801040426
42446CB00012B/2662